SMARTYpants
secrets

# NAMES and NAMING

*Names Have Great Power, to Help and to Hurt*

**D.R. Martin, PhD***
(*Personal human Development)

**SmartyPants Press**
Falmouth, Maine 04105
www.SmartyPantsSecrets.com

**ISBN 13: 978-1-943971-12-1**
**ISBN 10: 1943971129**

# The SmartyPants Secrets Concept

A **SmartyPants Secret** is that **one piece of information** that you need to know to make every job a little bit, or maybe a lot, **easier**. Almost everything we do in life has a SmartyPants secret that to it, that knowing the "secret" would help tremendously in shortening the learning curve.

After experiencing many "a ha!" moments that were previous head bangers, I realized that there was a lot of grief – i.e. aggravation, wasted time, spent resources - that could have been saved if I had known to tap into the insider information that others had and I was lacking. A SmartyPants secret is that crucial bit of timely knowledge.

We all want a magic bullet answer that solves all of our problems in one fell swoop and makes everything go perfectly well, preferably in record time!  We want that magic to happen right NOW, to be easily done, and to be preferably cheap, or at least not at great expense.  There are a lot of demands on our unattainable magic ☺

For example, one day I looked at my face and damn if I didn't see a "sun spot" (nastily also called a "liver" spot) marring the surface of my otherwise smooth face on the right lower cheek.  I scheduled an appointment at the dermatologist to verify the find and see if it could be lasered off. She sent me to an aesthetician who gave me some key information that made a huge difference in my decision of what to do next.

I was told that my even slightly darker (Asian) skin carries more pigment than Caucasian skin obviously. But what's not obvious is the way the body works, specifically the way the skin works, which is that when you wound the skin's surface, which laser surgery would certainly do, extra pigments rush to the spot to heal it (the "job" of pigment is to protect the underlying cells). The net result is that non-Caucasian skin heals into darker scabs and scars. (I have noticed this phenomena before but never made a direct connection.) Why then would I ever choose to have laser surgery on my face to remove a mark only to end up with an even darker mark? Yikes!

Obviously I wouldn't, but without this specialized knowledge about different results with different skin types, that even the dermatologist didn't know (yes, she was the recommender of the laser surgery option) I would've made a poor decision, with permanent negative results. A SmartyPants timely secret to the rescue!

Experts, who have hours of experience doing what the newbie is attempting to do, have expert knowledge, which may not be so secret, but it is **key information** that the novice greatly needs.

If you've ever struggled with something then learned the 'something' afterwards that caused you to say to yourself or to say aloud, "*Well, **if I only known THAT before I did this**, it would've made a world of difference!*" then you just learned a SmartyPants secret - the hard way.

The short SmartyPants Secrets books give you the secret that you need on a given topic, the most important piece of information that makes the greatest difference between easier success and hard-fought failure.

When I was young there was a professor at Cornell University, which in his obituary listed him as "***the last man to know everything***." I was taken by the concept of anyone knowing everything there is to know contained in one brain. Oh, to have such a mind!

But **to know everything**, logical facts and figures, and **to be able to do everything** are **two different things**. Brain power doesn't equal skill and expertise.

Today that one brain that knows everything is the Internet. There is so much information today available on the Internet; we can all be like that professor at Cornell and have access to all knowledge at the click of our fingertips.

More knowledge than we could ever consume - **who has time** to go through it all? Most of the time **what you really want is to know is the crux of the subject** on hand, not the whole litany of everything imaginable that is available to know.

***Tell me just what I need to know!*** (and I likely don't know what specific knowledge to ask for). It's literally impossible to know what you don't know. Let the expertise of knowledgeable others guide you.

If you are new to a topic the **SmartyPants secret can save you time and effort**, which are important to your success. Not a complete course on the topic, which you can certainly get elsewhere, the SmartyPants secrets concept is primarily to help you **not miss the key information needed for success**.

The building block of knowledge that the foundation rests upon; the Keystone or cornerstone knowledge makes a critical difference, especially when that knowledge that you do have, or think you have, is **faulty, incomplete or missing** entirely.

The concept of **social proof** states that when we have no prior experience in a given situation we rely on **others to show us the way**. We believe that lacking personal knowledge, that their situation is similar to our situation, and therefore what worked for them has a high probability of working for us.

We quiz others about our shared circumstances around the situation to verify that their solution is a good one.  Plus, we think: *there's nothing to lose in trying since I don't have a better answer*.

Then when what worked for another doesn't happen to work for us, we are reminded that **we are all different people**, with different variables that impact success or failure.  Some solutions to problems are hit or miss depending on who we are. And sometimes success depends on having and following the right key knowledge.

**Solving problems is not the complete SmartyPants concept**, although SmartyPants secrets can indeed offer real help for real problems. Rather the full concept is that having that key knowledge piece makes efforts easier and successful quicker; hopefully **avoiding having the problem in the first place**. We do anything in life because we have a goal to achieve. Reaching that goal successfully, quickly and easier than without knowing the SmartPants secret is the SmartyPants concept.

And because **all SmartyPants secrets have a physiological root**, grounded in our shared human biology, every SmartyPants secret is valid for everyone, no matter who you are. While we are all uniquely different from each other, we have a **common biology** consisting of inherited traits that stretch back to the Neanderthal era.

Applying a SmartyPants secret **will work for you no matter who you are**. And in our busy world, who doesn't want to save time and know the SmartyPants secret to anything?

## *Why ever risk hindering easier success by not knowing the core success secret?*

# What's In a Name?

Shakespeare wrote in the play <u>Romeo and Juliet</u> *"a rose by any other name would smell as sweet"*.

But in reality  the connotation of sweetness is embodied in the word itself exactly because it was given the name "rose".

Being so named, now anything also called "rose", be it a girl' s name or a paint color, carries that same sweet quality.  We don't think of 'rose' as anything else except fragrant and lovely.

Names, like all words, are nothing more than a **string of consonant and vowels** that are attached together without rationale.

What is a '**Jane**' or a '**John**' exactly?  While we perhaps know people with those names, there is no '*Jane-ness*' that we can attach to the name; we do attach certain qualities with names that are also attached to physical **tangible objects**, like a rose.

People whose names are found in nature - with names like **Violet, June, Frank, Jack** - are easier to remember because we can **associate a visual image** with the name.

Names that have no tangible counterpart rely on **rote memory** to recall. This is true whether it is the first name or last name we are trying to recall - names are hard to remember because there is **no logical association** between the person in their name.

In every culture there are names, that random mix of consonants and vowels, that are recognized as being names that people call their children, or their pets, or their prized possessions that they choose to name. The process of naming **assigns an identity, usually of high-value and affection**, for the item/person.

Naming is important - actually very important - because of the **self-identity** that is embodied in a person's name. Although one's name is usually not self-selected, it is defended and offense is taken as a **personal insult** when someone's good name is marred. We may not have chosen it, but our parents did, we believe lovingly, so we take pride in it as our first and foremost identity.

We hear our names across a noisy room; our ears pick up when our name is spoken, sweet music to hear. We make mention when somebody's name is the same as one of our loved ones, conferring to them a specialness, illogically making them extra special because they share a name with one of our beloveds.

What's in a name? Quite a bit - so be sure to **get the person's name right**, get the exactly **correct spelling**, and use it as their favorite word, since it's a personal reflection of self-identity.

# Foreign Names are Tough

All the lovely plants and flowers that grow in a garden have scientific formal names with a Latin base that most people don't know, don't care to know, and certainly don't remember; plants go by their common names instead - foreign names are tough!

We used to live on **Olde Birch Lane** - or should I say, **Olde Betula Lane**.  It was named because of the white birch trees, more accurately *betula papyrifera* (which my spellcheck hates!) . We now live on **Red Oak Drive**, which is - you guessed it - more accurately **Quercus Rubra Drive** (not to be confused with **Quercus Coccinea Drive**! - which is more accurately *Spanish Oak,* or *scarlet oak*).

And what about all the names - **generic and brand names - for medications/drug** prescriptions?  Those who need their meds have learned the various drug names that they need, but those names don't exactly roll off the uninitiated tongue easily.  Medicinal names are largely based on Greek sources  - the expression *it's Greek to me* is quite accurate here.

$$\alpha\beta\gamma\delta$$
$$\varepsilon\zeta\eta\theta$$

I am easily perplexed and have a hard time remembering the names and uses of a laundry list of drugs that many older people take on a daily basis.  It's confusing and just plain hard to remember drug names until you're used to them.

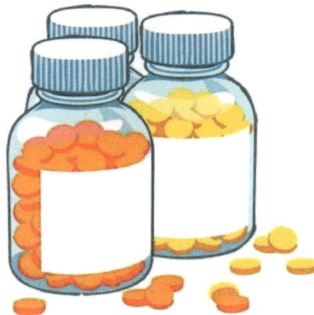

Since every culture has its own language and every language has its own set of random consonants and vowels that are put together in agreed-upon packages called names, when we are not familiar with these combinations it's even **harder to remember foreign names**, especially when we **do not speak the language**.

Sometimes we have a hard time even pronouncing someone's foreign name because the consonant vowel combinations are **not patterns that our tongues are familiar with**. And the name memorization process becomes even more difficult when trying to remember several word patterns that sound odd to our ears.

People who come to live in other countries and learn their language are just as proud of their names as everyone else, so they may not choose to change their given name to an English name that is easier for their new English-speaking neighbors to remember.

The exception to this is people who come from China (the world's most populous country) where a different alphabet (characters instead of letters) prevents a literal rendering of the name into English. Often these individuals will take an English first name.  But because the Chinese family surname is the most important, it is usually translated from Chinese to an English equivalent and maintained with pride.

Many of our towns and landmarks have foreign name roots, since only the Native Americans were here originally, and they didn't speak English.  Some of their assigned names for towns, and natural landmarks, like rivers, lakes and islands, have stuck, but many were renamed over time.  Like **Noepe**, which means "***land amid the streams***" in **Wampanoag**, which we famously know today as Martha's Vineyard.

## *Noepe → renamed: Martha's Vineyard*

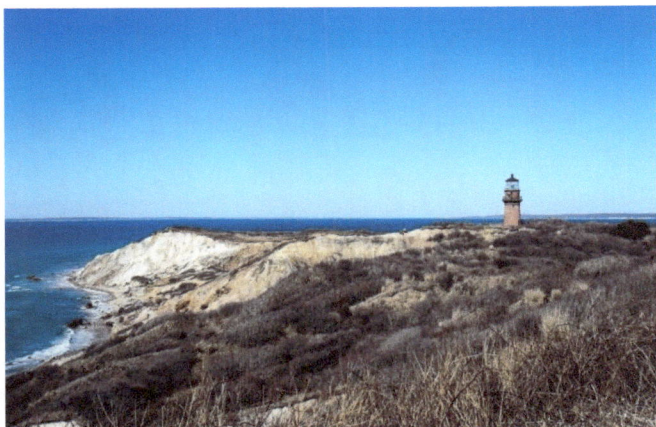

# The Persona Of a Person's Name

In the TV show Mad Men the lead character, **Don Draper**, was really born **Dick Whitman**. When he was Don, he was a very dapper executive with a persona that fit. When he was Dick, he was a different person. When we take on a name we take on an **associated identity**.

A friend retired to Georgia and decided she would change her name for her new community and retirement life. She picked the name **Cookie** as a suitable new name and promptly introduced herself to everyone she met in Georgia with that new name. Soon she took on the persona of Cookie, which she could sculpt to be anything she wanted it to be. **New life, new name** - why not?

## 1st 50 years: Brenda → 2nd 50 years: Cookie

Actors, performance artists, authors understand this concept well. A chosen name can strongly impact professional success. Just ask Marion Morrison (John Wayne) or Norma Mortenson (Marilyn Monroe)

# Sticks and Stones May Break My Bones, But (Calling) Names Will Never Hurt Me

This old children's rhyme is true in the physical sense of the word 'hurt', but so untrue in the emotional hurt that's inflicted with **verbal abuse that name-calling** is.

We may think that giving someone an unpleasant nickname is just all in good fun, but the hurt can cut to the quick, especially **when the name is never wanted, liked or downright offensive**. Sometimes a nickname sticks for many years and is hard to shake.  With families, old nicknames that are carried into adulthood can be nearly impossible to change.

While most live with their nickname, and don't even hear the insult after a while, still the **psychological damage is done after years of enduring the derogatory label**.

A grandfather that in jest routinely calls his beloved granddaughter "***pest***" can't help but have influence on the developing child, that has been called a pest since she was a toddler!

A heavyweight adult with the nickname "**Chub**", which he has carried his whole life and introduces himself with that name, is a **self-filling prophecy**. While jovial and friendly, Chub clearly never prioritized his health as important.

The father who had twin sons, naming one son **Winner** and the other son **Loser** thought that the naming of children was *just a big joke*. Unfortunately those children carried those real names with them throughout their life, with all the accompanying hardships that those names brought. It's hard enough to be a child growing up with peer pressure without the extra burden of an oddball name.

*Which one did Winner grow up to be? And what about Loser as a grownup?*

[Real life social experiment ending: *Winner, picked on and harassed, grew up to be a tough criminal; Lou grew up to be a police officer.*]

# NICKNAMES

We give someone a favorable nickname usually as a term of endearment, bringing us closer to the person.  Nicknames can also serve as a shortcut when the name is just too troublesome to remember or pronounce. "Auntie" shortens to "tee" to a young tongue.

Without the ease of a nickname, we might **butcher the name** over and over again..

Or we just don't like our given name, so nickname ourselves. A friend named Walter called himself Butch.  Then he carried on the disliked first name to his own son, with young Walter Jr going by Skip. (Parents - duh!)

Some common nicknames are based on last names.  Tom Weiser was called Bud.  Many with the last name of O'Brien go by Obie. Shortening the last name is very typical - Mitch Mitchell is really David Mitchell (Jimi Hendrix's drummer), but certainly not the only Mitch Mitchell.  Other last names lend themselves to offensive nicknames, especially for males: Hancock, Dixon, Horner.

# Oldest known relative, *Lucy*

Or should I say: **Australopithecus afarensis** – yowzer, that's a mouthful!  No wonder we call her Lucy!

*Dear old Great, Great, Great...[insert 1.8 million years of great]... Great Aunt Lucy.*

# George Foreman and His Five Sons

When you have five sons and you don't want to remember all of their names, it's easiest just to give them all the same name, which is what George Foreman did, **naming all his sons after himself, George**.

But when you have six George Foremans in the

same family, naturally nicknames are created so other people and family members know which George they're talking about at any given time.  Since nicknames tend to rule, having the same name became a non-issue, except legally.

## *George Foreman - "Big George"*

## *George Foreman Jr – "Junior"*

## *George Foreman III – "Monk"*

## *George Foreman VI – "Big Wheel"*

## *George Foreman V – "Red"*

## *George Foreman VI –  "Little Joey"*

Since a name is so personal, a nickname is even more so and reserved for those who are closest to the person.  **Never assume a person's nickname, or that you can use it without their permission.**

When meeting  Mr. Michael Smith, instead of asking, *"Do you go by Mike?"* or *"I hear that your friends call you Smitty, would that be best for me to use?",* rather you should inquire, *"What do you prefer to be called?"* and let him tell you. Now you have permission, or not, but at least you have guidance.

Some people prefer to their formal name and **abhor nicknames** of any kind for themselves. My college roommate was named **Kathleen**; since there were Kathys aplenty back then, the preferred nickname for Kathleen, I just assumed that she went by **Kathy**, and penned my introductory letter accordingly. Wrong! She quickly wrote back that it was *Kathleen*, addressing the name issue right out of the gate. I never did that again, and helped correct others that freshman year who made the same mistake with her name.

Patricia also goes by Patricia. But another **Patricia** that I know went by **Pat** for many years. One day she mentioned that her family calls her **Trish**. I asked what she preferred to be called, since I knew her as Pat - she answered "Trish" - so to that date forward she was Trish to all of our friends.

It's not easy to change verbal habits when you've been calling somebody by a certain name for years, then find out that they prefer a different name.  But when you ask the name question and receive back a different answer than you were expecting, you should accommodate.

A book club friend we had all been calling **Ginny** for years, when asked her name preference, replied "**Virginia**".  Formal given names stand out in a world of nicknames.

I have always called my husband Michael, although he introduces himself to everyone else as Mike. "Michael" is a special pet name for my use only, and now after decades I can't change the habit.

# Cutesy Funny Names

**Mr. and Mrs. Hand** named their daughter **Linda**.

The Rachels who liked their last name so much they also named their middle daughter Rachel. (Certainly easy to remember, thinking along the same lines as George Foreman?)

This is not an uncommon practice: Thomas Thomas, James James, and Rose Rose are the most common occurrences of 'double names'. William Williams, Edward Edwards, Andy

Andrews, Tony Anthony, Chris Christie among others with a version of name doubling.

It's not unusual for people who have never liked their given first name to go to court, pay a moderate fee, and have their name changed to something more to their liking.

There is **Mr. Time** who legally changed his first name to **Justin**. Or a childhood friend went from 'Julia' to 'Daphne' in middle school, then made it legal as an adult.

A bad example of parents thinking that they're being funny (or perhaps they were just lazy namers?) is the child named **Abcde** – pronounced like *obesity, accept with an "A"*. Really, how mean is that to do to a child?

Also difficult is when parents name boys with traditional girl names. **Ashley**, for instance, was not always feminine, but is certainly that way now. **Leslie, Shannon** and **Kelly** are other examples.

It used to be that the male and female spelling of the same sounding name told you the gender: **Marian** for the female version and **Marion** for the male version; **Frances** and **Francis**; perhaps **Lindsey** and **Lindsay**. But with all the unusual spelling of all kinds of names today, that 'rule' is hardly enforceable. My mom was Marion, born in 1909; Nana and Papa were hardly mavericks.

Remember the female actress **Michael Learned**, mom on The Waltons? How about females named **Ryan**? Males named **Courtney**? When a child is named with a **name that is commonly attributed to the other gender**, there are many assumptions and associations, plus a lifetime burden of correcting people.

This also happens when a name has a **strange pronunciation or is spelled in an unusual way**. Unintentionally, I ended up strapping my daughter with having to repeatedly announce, "*It's pronounced* **'Kelani'**, *like Melanie with a K*"; I thought I was giving her a lovely name instead of a lifetime chore of correcting strangers.

Then there are those that purposely choose an unusual pronunciation of their name to stand out. The rapper Flo Rida. The Da-vids of the world. Sheesh, correctly pronouncing some names can be a real minefield. And correct pronunciation is important to strive for.

# Last Name Issues

Some last names can be troublesome, especially for kids in school with peer pressure issues, but then there's that name pride thing, so parents assume that it builds character for kids to suffer through it.  To mature adults last names are rarely problematic.  It's the grade school years when other kids give them a hard time that may leave an emotional mark.

William Hore decided not to put his future children through unnecessary torment so before he married and fathered four kids he went to court and simply slid an s in the front of a proud Anglo-Saxon name that has changed in connotation over time, transforming the unwanted **Hore** to an inoffensive **Shore**.

Similarly evolved negative connotations have affected names like Gross, Butts, Harr, Butcher, Weiner, Boozer – it's hard to take peer ribbing when you're young.  And poor **Lorna Boozer**, growing up when *Pig Latin* was all the rage...

*Borna Loozer*

With family pride of names, more and more women are not taking their husbands surname, with any children receiving a hyphenated last name, making for some long unwieldy last name combinations.

Since there are school pickup issues and feeling like a family, many millennial parents opt for the hyphenated solution, which is similar to the practice of making the mother's last name as the children's middle name. Same concept, without the hyphen.

In China the last name is most important and carries all the weight; the surname goes first which is the opposite of in Western culture where the surname is last. Surnames are so important in China's male-dominated culture that traditionally the males carry their father's surname and the females carry their mother's surname. Over centuries and generations this practice has fragmented Chinese last names; certain males names are the coveted high-valued names to marry into, with certain corresponding female surnames commonly regarded with disdain.

臺灣台湾

# First Names

## Name Meaning

When most people select a first name for their child, they usually go by the melodic sound of the name as a *sound that they like*, or after a person that they like; few people look up the meaning of the name or care what the name supposedly means.  Several names have negative meanings, but who really knows or cares?

Claudia – "lame"    Kennedy–"misshapen head"
`
Deirdre – "sorrowful"     Blaise – "lisp, stutter"

Leah – "weary"                Calvin – "bald"

Mallory – "unlucky"   Cameron –"crooked nose"

Persephone –"bringing      Gideon – "having a
            Death"                    stump hand"

Cecilia – "blind"    Campbell – "crooked mouth"

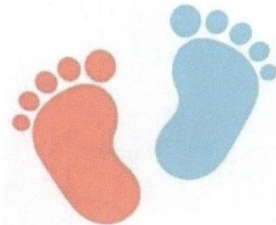

# SELECTION

Several people name their children with family first names that are passed down through the generations.  This pride in family is perpetuated in the naming process, that frequently honors a relative, deceased or living.

Another common practice is to make mothers surname the middle name for the children. This honors both surnames, when the fathers surname is the family last name.

And some first names are combination of different names.  **Cybill Shepherd** comes to mind, named after two uncles **Cy** and **Bill**.

My old best friend in elementary school was named **Rona Lee**, which was her mother **Eleanor**'s name largelyspelled backwards.

In old China they would name babies purposely with an unimportant first name, picking a minor object that is not boastful in nature, feeling that the gods would take no notice to harm a child with a trivial name like Little Tree.

# Cultural /Ethnic Name Stereotyping

Some names sound very ethnic – **Jamaal, Lakisha** - which then stereotypes the person, for good or for bad.  Studies have shown that it is nearly impossible for adults not to be influenced by their perceptions, which names carry.

**José Zamora** learned this lesson when he applied to hundreds of jobs and received zero response until he changed his resume to **Joe Zamora** - the first name made all the difference; the resume interest picked right up.

A study in San Diego with 80 teachers across 10 elementary schools revealed the power of names on grades.  Submitted compositions received lower school grades when the name on the top of the paper was **Bertha versus Lisa or Karen.**  The highest grades went to **Adelia**.  With boys, the same results occurred with the perceived male loser names **of Elmer and Hubert**, who were bested on the exact same work by **David and Michael.**  The conclusion was that popular names were smarter than perceived dumb names, and those with highly unusual names (i.e.

Adelia) were less popular socially with their peers and therefore **more studious**. The additional conclusion was that boys with loser names were likely taunted by their peers, making them aggressive and antagonistic towards teachers, therefore not studious.

Whether this bears truth today or not, with all the unusual names and unusual spellings that parents create their children, it bears mention when selecting the child's name.

### *Top 10 names in 1950
(*based on social security records)

| GIRL | BOY |
| --- | --- |
| Mary | James |
| Patricia | John |
| Jennifer | Robert |
| Elizabeth | Michael |
| Linda | William |
| Barbara | David |
| Susan | Richard |
| Margaret | Joseph |
| Jessica | Charles |
| Sarah | Thomas |

*Fast forward 65 years...*

## *Top 10 names in 2015

| GIRL | BOY |
|------|-----|
| Sophia | Jackson |
| Emma | Aiden |
| Olivia | Liam |
| Ava | Lucas |
| Isabella | Noah |
| Mia | Mason |
| Zoe | Ethan |
| Lily | Caden |
| Emily | Logan |
| Madison | Jacob |

## Top 10 Upper Class** Names

| GIRL | BOY |
|------|-----|
| Charlotte | Henry |
| Seraphina | Finn |
| **Olivia** | Oliver |
| Elizabeth | James |
| Lucy | Asher |
| Isla | **Jack** |
| Violet | Jasper |
| **Sophia** | Max |
| Alice | Kai |
| Maisie | Atticus |

(**names often originate in the upper class, then when in common usage, are dropped by the upper class as too common, i.e. Brittany)

## Versions of the Same Basic Name

Kathleen, Katie, Kathryn, Kay, Koo, Kot, Katherine, Kath, Kaitlin, Kathy, Kayla, Kailee, Kate, Kati, Katy, Kaylee, Kayleigh  (then all the variations beginning with 'C' start...)

# Name Merchandise

Retailers understand the fixation, pride, and self-identity that go along with hearing and seeing your name in print for children; they mass-produce any number of products imprinted with common names - pencils, rulers, hair barrettes, mini pads of paper, small bike vanity plates, etc. Even Coca-Cola recently printed common names on individual bottles of Coke. Get ready for the tears when your unusually named child laments, *"they never have my name..."* or *"they never have the correct spelling of my name!"*

Peer pressure makes kids want to fit in and not be different. When they can't blend in with the crowd because their name is not a common one and they can't buy merchandise stamped with their name that the top names can avail themselves of; well, at least they're building good character!

# New Role?  New Name!

Whenever you get a new family role you have the chance to consider what name you want to take.  This usually occurs when a child marries and you are now a **mother-in-law or a father-in-law.**

When you become a **grandparent** is another opportunity to select a name for yourself.  (A label that a friend coined which I love is "grandsister" - the relationship of a grandmother with the other grandmother.)

In China there is a name for every position in a family, with a different word for not only a paternal relative versus a maternal relative, but also the placement of the relative in their own family.  So you know by the role name exactly what position that person is –third aunt on their mother's side.  Very specific linguistics that English lacks.

So what is the new son-in-law or daughter-in-law going to call you?  'Mom' and 'Dad' have an emotion attached that not everyone is willing to extend, even as an honor, aside from their own parents, depending on what those labels connote to each person.

I had this very dilemma, marrying at 19 and not knowing what to call my new in-laws. Calling them by their first name felt disrespectful; 'Mr' and 'Mrs' was too formal; 'Mom' and 'Dad' was out of the question for me.  Since I was too young to anticipate this problem and since my in-laws didn't address it either, we went for years without a resolution until it finally became too late to bring it up.

Through the years I would talk to my in-laws by either making eye contact, or touching them lightly to get their attention and then speaking to them.  I refer to them in the third person as "my husband's parents" or with my children refer to them by their grandparent names.  Several decades later, with the name issue still unresolved, I decided when it was my turn that this name lacking history would not repeat itself.

Since I knew that my children marrying would bring up the grandparent name issue I decided to come up with a name that could be used by both grandchildren and son/daughter-in-laws alike. It is a unique name to our family which means 'grandmother' and I know that it only refers to me when it's used.

There are several traditional names that people take to mean 'grandparent', typically a name they used for their own grandparents. But you still have the chance to select your own name, something of your own choosing based on your comfort level. It's a decision to give some thought to because names have power, embodied a persona and do not have to be the default choice.

If Granny or Grammy feels too old for you, why default to it?  If instead Grammie feels like an honor that you've earned, then wear it proudly.  The point is to give it some thought and **choose** – something that wraps comfortably around you for years to come.

If you let the default option happen due to inertia, and years down the road think, "I never liked that name, but that's what I ended up stuck with" well then, see the future happening now and do something about it!

You get to decide what people call you throughout your life.  It's never too late to go with what's really comfortable for you.

# Naming Pets

So you have new pooch, Kitty, rabbit, or other domesticated animal that is coming to live with you and must be named. The beauty of pets is that they don't know or care what kind of name you choose to give them, so no harm/no foul with choosing a stupid, funny, or crass name for your new pet.

The dog name Sex. The cat named Cat. Katy Purry, Walter Croncat, Purrcilla, Barkley, Zippity Do Dawg – all great pet names.

In fact, there are really no bad pet names. Clever meaningful names reflect the personal tastes of the owner. My daughter named her little 2 pound teacup Yorkie "Penny Lane", Penny for short; with a nod to the Beatles, and perfect for her small physical size.

(Rule of thumb: do not name any animal that will become dinner at any future date…)

# Naming Large Possessions

## HOMES

People may think that they need to have massive estates with lots of passed down family land to name their home - not true! The home is typically the biggest most valued possession that people have - why not give it a name?  Yet few people do so.

Naming something indicates that it's cherished. Building our new home was a labor of love that spanned 18 months (quoted as taking six months, ha!) and turned out beautifully.  We named her "Eudora", which means "good gift".

My daughter bought a starter home, not her last home for sure but still worthy of a name. She named it "Hattie", which means "ruler of the home".  I had a plaque made for her, which she will likely bring to her new home, which will also be named Hattie.

You cherish the place you call home; so why haven't you named it yet?

# BOATS

Boats always get named, usually with female names, but sometimes with idyllic or humorous expressions.

Traditionally the boat's name served the utilitarian function of designating which sailing vessel passengers were boarding.

Today boat naming is done purely for ego since there is no utilitarian need to name a boat.

But as a cherished possession a boat is certainly worthy and deserving of a name, if you happen to own one.

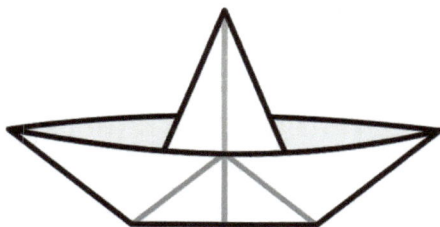

# CARS, TRUCKS, GUITARS

Cars and trucks are also commonly named, and also commonly left unnamed. The easier way to label a car is on a vanity license plate, which is not a name but a clever sentiment.

So there is no real need to name a vehicle, which is usually designated by the make or model name, unless of course you want to give it its own affectionate name or nickname.

My sister's first car was a yellow wagon named Buttercup. Buttercup didn't last that long and she hasn't named any subsequent cars.

But for those who are very attached to their vehicles, or any other large treasured possession, a name is a nice term of endearment. And we do tend to treat things better that we name.

*Willie Nelson and Lucille*

# BUSINESSES/Business Products

Naming a business is an important decision with many considerations to factor in the naming process.

Clever business names are fun, but clarity is most important.  For Us All, Inc., Save Day, Inc., Captain 401, Inc -  unclear what they do.

Naming retail products is also key to success with consumers buying those products.  No matter how delicious, I'm going to have a hard time with soup named 'Placenta'...or 'Soup for Sluts'!

A hot tea Romanian drink named 'Urinal' is also a hard sell.  And did anyone bother to check the translation and think it might be a good idea to re-name the Japanese snack, 'Only Puke', for English speaking markets?

# The SmartyPants Secret on NAMES

**A name has deep effects on our psyche at an unconscious level, impacting our perceptions and others' perceptions, favorably or unfavorably.**

Much more than "just" a name; names hold great power.

*Select yours wisely and intentionally.*

# BOOK BUYER BONUS

As a thank you to buyers, there is an additional free resource available only to book buyers. Did you get yours?  If you missed it, go to www.SmartyPantsSecrets.com/bookbonus .

It's has additional valuable content and is free to book buyers, so don't miss out on getting yours!

# ABOUT

I am DR Martin, PhD* (*Personal human
Development expertise) – Dolley Rapoport
Martin.  I took Dolley as my first name* in
honor of the great First Lady Dolley Madison,
whom I admire for her heroic actions in the
White House during very turbulent times.

I took Rapoport as a middle name* in honor of
Ingeborg Rapoport, who at age 103, is the
oldest person to be awarded a Doctorate;
finally getting the recognition due her from 77
years prior in Nazi Germany, unfairly denied
her due to her Jewish roots.  There is so much
injustice in the world; it is an honor to
recognize her achievement by taking her
name, the importance of which is further
explained in this book.

I have studied every communication subject
for more than a decade, acquiring a large body
of knowledge.  I, perhaps like you, am a
voracious reader and learner.  My other
strength is that I retain much of what I learn,
so I can then compile the knowledge on a
variety of subjects into a concise format,
making the books that I author a shortcut on

the best knowledge available.  This saves you from going through all the data looking for the kernel that makes the greatest difference in success, the SmartyPants secret on a given topic.

I also have a mind that is ever curious about so many topics.  I have earned multiple expert designations (education certified English teacher, Real Estate Broker, Stock Broker series 7, series 6, series, Certified Financial Manager, Insurance producer certified, Coach University) and held high level positions in business – large corporate entities, privately held companies, non-profit organizations, and startups  – and have volunteered extensively, holding executive positions at the local, district and national levels.  So I've been around the block more than once, on more than one topic.

Due to my research and experience, I have logged the perquisite time to carry the title of expert, giving myself an honorary PhD in the expertise area of communication, Personal human Development.  I am passionate about sharing the knowledge that I have gained with you, in bite-size pieces.

And when a certain topic is not in my field of expertise, I find an expert with deep expertise in the field who has the knowledge that I seek. I then ask numerous in-depth questions of the expert to get to the gist, learn the SmartyPants Secret, to then pass the knowledge on in a book on the subject.

SMARTY**pants**
secrets

For other titles and additional resources, visit
www.SmartyPantsSecrets.com

All book titles at www.amazon.com/-/e/B018HA35I8

Watch for content clips and helpful technique tips on a variety of topics coming soon at
www.youtube.com/c/smartypantssecrets

Contact: Info@SmartyPantsSecrets.com

www.ingramcontent.com/pod-product-compliance
Lightning Source LLC
Chambersburg PA
CBHW041226270326
41934CB00001B/16